1 Thessalonians

30-DAY DEVOTIONAL

1 Thessalonians

Alec Motyer
with Elizabeth McQuoid

FOOD
FOR THE
JOURNEY

INTER-VARSITY PRESS
36 Causton Street, London SW1P 4ST, England
Email: ivp@ivpbooks.com
Website: www.ivpbooks.com

First published 2016

British Library Cataloguing-in-Publication Data
A catalogue record for this book is available from the British Library.

ISBN: 978-1-78359-439-9
eBook ISBN: 978-1-78359-503-7

Typeset in Great Britain by CRB Associates, Potterhanworth, Lincolnshire
Printed in Great Britain by Ashford Colour Press Ltd, Gosport, Hampshire

Preface

Can you guess how many sermons have been preached from the Keswick platform? Almost 6,500!

For over 140 years, the Keswick Convention in the English Lake District has welcomed gifted expositors from all over the world. The convention's archive is a treasure trove of sermons preached on every book of the Bible.

This series is an invitation to mine that treasure. It takes talks from the Bible Reading series given by well-loved Keswick speakers, past and present, and reformats them into daily devotionals. Where necessary, the language has been updated but, on the whole, it is the message you would have heard had you been listening in the tent on Skiddaw Street. Each day of the devotional ends with a newly written section designed to help you apply God's Word to your own life and situation.

Whether you are a convention regular or have never been to Keswick, this Food for the Journey series provides a unique opportunity to study the Scriptures with a Bible teacher by your side. Each book is designed to fit in your jacket pocket or handbag so you can read it anywhere – over the breakfast table, on the commute into work or college, while you are waiting in your car, during your lunch break or in bed at night. Wherever life's journey takes you, time in God's Word is vital nourishment for your spiritual journey.

Our prayer is that these devotionals become your daily feast, a precious opportunity to meet with God through his Word. Read, meditate, apply and pray through the Scriptures given for each day, and allow God's truths to take root and transform your life.

If these devotionals whet your appetite for more, there is a 'For further study' section at the end of each book. You can also visit our website at www.keswickministries.org/resources to find the full range of books, study guides, CDs, DVDs and mp3s available. Why not order an audio recording of the Bible Reading series to accompany your daily devotional?

Let the word of Christ dwell in you richly.
(Colossians 3:16, ESV)

1 Thessalonians

'Keep on pressing on'.

Do you need to hear these words today?

'Keep on pressing on' was the theme of the first letter Paul ever wrote. It was a message that the Thessalonians, and every believer since, has needed to hear.

Paul visited Thessalonica, a bustling commercial seaport, on his second mission trip, along with his companions Silas and Timothy. As was his custom, Paul preached in the synagogue and a number of Jews, as well as many Gentiles and some prominent women, accepted the gospel. Unfortunately, the visit was cut short after only four or five weeks when Paul was hounded out of the city by Jewish opposition (Acts 17:1–9).

But, amazingly, by the time he left, there was a fledgling church.

Paul wrote to these new believers to fill in details and explain misunderstandings about the second coming, to urge them to live well in Christian community and to give further instructions about godly living, all the while encouraging them to press on in holiness regardless of outside opposition. His prayer for them was that they would become all that they ought to be in character and conduct.

Whatever age or stage of the Christian life you are, whatever circumstances you are facing, Paul's message to 'Keep on pressing on' is for you. Let the encouragements, challenges and truths from 1 Thessalonians spur you on in your spiritual journey, so that, like these New Testament believers, we would become all that we ought to be in character and conduct.

Day 1

Read 1 Thessalonians 1:1–10
Key verse: 1 Thessalonians 1:1

....

¹Paul, Silas and Timothy,
To the church of the Thessalonians in God the Father and the Lord Jesus Christ:
Grace and peace to you.

Complete the phrase, 'I'm in . . .' What is the first word that comes into your mind? Perhaps your answer was: 'I'm in work', 'I'm in hospital', 'I'm in university', 'I'm in pain' or simply 'I'm in a rush'!

Although each of us faces different scenarios, there is a banner that can be put over the life of every Christian: we are 'in God the Father and the Lord Jesus Christ'.

When we become Christians, God, like a careful gardener, gently takes us out of the habitat in which we were living, and he transplants us into himself. Our union with him means that we are planted into a system perfectly suited to the new nature we have been given, specially designed to cultivate our growth, development and fruitfulness.

Remember the image of the vine and the branches Jesus used in John 15? The branches are in a system perfectly designed to maintain their health, growth and fruitfulness. We are also in a system perfectly designed for our holiness, development and usefulness. We have been planted into God the Father and the Lord Jesus Christ. And all the life of God the Father and God the Son, bound together as one God, surround us as soon as we become Christians. His life is there for us to put our roots into and draw our nourishment from, so that we grow straight, true, clean and fruitful.

Did you notice Paul gives Jesus his full title in this verse? Paul doesn't want us to miss the amazing nature and privilege of our union. We are united with the Lord, God himself. He comes to us not only as Lord but as Jesus, the one who understands us and can perfectly minister to our needs. And he comes as Christ, the one who was anointed to be the totally perfect Saviour of sinners.

Are you beginning to feel like a protected species? Are you beginning to realize how precious you are to God?

It is easy to look at life simply from an earthly per-spective: we are 'in a family crisis', 'in a reshuffle at work', 'in remission' or sometimes just 'in a rush'. But consider the difference it makes to see your life from God's perspective: you are 'in God the Father and the Lord Jesus Christ'. The breath-taking miracle of your salvation means you are now united with God. You have his life to strengthen you, his Word to nourish you, his Spirit to guide you. Meditate on the image of the vine and the branches from John 15. Be a Psalm 1 believer:

Blessed is the one . . .
whose delight is in the law of the LORD,
    and who meditates on his law day and night.
That person is like a tree planted by streams of water,
    which yields its fruit in season
and whose leaf does not wither –
    whatever they do prospers.

Sink your roots deep into Christ today.

Day 2

Read 1 Thessalonians 1:1–10
Key verse: 1 Thessalonians 1:1

....

¹Paul, Silas and Timothy,
*   To the church of the Thessalonians in God the*
Father and the Lord Jesus Christ:
*   Grace and peace to you.*

What do you think you most need, to grow as a Christian? Sometimes we imagine we would be able to make better strides as disciples if only God were more explicit with his guidance, quicker to answer our prayers and keener to change our circumstances. But God's means of growth is to nourish us with his grace and peace.

Grace is not something God gives; not something he hands out like medicine. There is no such thing as grace apart from God. Grace is God being gracious. It is the free, undeserved, unmerited movement of God sharing himself with his people as our Father and as our Lord Jesus Christ. Our salvation was an act of sheer grace

(Ephesians 2:4–5). And now, through Jesus' death, God offers us the perfect setting to live and grow, in union with him. There we find God's fatherly love, saving mercy and eternal power surrounding us.

He also offers us peace. Of course, peace begins with a restored relationship with God. But peace also means 'peace and fulfilment in our own being'. When God ministers peace to us, he is ministering to us all those things that bring us to fulfilment and full maturity: peace with God; the peace of a truly fulfilled humanity; peace in society; peace in fellowship with our Christian brothers and sisters. God's peace, his *shalom*, is not simply the absence of war but also the wholeness, well-being, rest and contentment that we experience when we live in union with him.

What are the 'extras' you are looking for to speed up your Christian growth? Are you waiting for clearer guidance, better circumstances or even deeper spiritual experiences? Stop! God has given you everything you need to grow as a disciple: he has given you himself. Your union with God is a treasure store, containing all you will ever need for life and godliness. You first became aware of God's grace and peace when you were saved. But that was just the beginning! Experiencing

God's grace and peace daily nourishes your faith and helps it grow. Give thanks today for all the evidence of God's grace in your life and rest in his peace, knowing your wholeness and well-being are not wrapped up in your achievements, but only and always in Christ.

Day 3

Read 1 Thessalonians 1:1–10
Key verses: 1 Thessalonians 1:2–3

....

²We always thank God for all of you and continually mention you in our prayers. ³We remember before our God and Father your work produced by faith, your labour prompted by love, and your endurance inspired by hope in our Lord Jesus Christ.

When people look at you, what do they make of your life? Is it obvious from your actions and behaviour that you are a Christian?

In Thessalonica, the young believers were already bearing fruit. They were only weeks old in the faith and yet the evidence of their new life was obvious. John the Baptist once said, 'Produce fruit in keeping with repentance' (Matthew 3:8). And Paul is echoing his point. If we are truly repentant, it will show; spiritual experience is a matter not of claim but of evidence. And being fruitful isn't for the few, it isn't for some time in the future; it is something that happens from the moment we are saved. We demonstrate our new life in Christ by our faith in God, our love for others and our hope in Jesus' return.

Notice that Paul doesn't apologize to the Thessalonians that their faith required hard work and endurance. He assumes it is quite normal that being a Christian is demanding. However, when we face struggles, we are often quick to wonder, 'What is God thinking about?' Well, he is thinking about the fact that he calls us to live by faith, to live in love and to exercise hope. He is calling us to be what we are. The troubles and toils of life which demand faith, hard work and endurance are not unnatural experiences. They are the conditions God chooses for our growth.

Circumstances may be difficult and you may feel very weary, but don't give up. Hold on to faith: faith in Christ saved you, so trust him with every difficulty you face today. Hold on to love: keep on loving your church family in practical, self-sacrificing ways. Hold on to hope: endure each day knowing that one day soon Jesus is coming back. Remember, struggles are good soil for growth, so don't waste them! Pray that your perseverance and fruitfulness will point someone to Jesus today.

Day 4

Read 1 Thessalonians 1:1–10
Key verses: 1 Thessalonians 1:4–5

. . . .

⁴For we know, brothers and sisters loved by God, that he has chosen you, ⁵because our gospel came to you not simply with words but also with power, with the Holy Spirit and deep conviction. You know how we lived among you for your sake.

My friend was explaining to her adopted daughter how loved and precious she was. So she said, 'Other mums and dads just have to accept whatever child they get, but we *chose* you.'

Out of God's great love he *chose* us. God looked at us and said, 'Yes, I want that one.' We may worry: 'What about my choice? Didn't I choose Jesus to be my Saviour?' Well, we need to remember that we were 'dead in [our] transgressions and sins' (Ephesians 2:1). We couldn't even exercise repentance and faith: we were spiritually dead, without a spark of life. 'But because of his great love for us, God, who is rich in mercy, made us alive with Christ' (Ephesians 2:4–5). God had to take the initiative. There is no way we can come to life in Christ until he first gives us life. And he gave us life, simply because he loved us.

So what happened? How does salvation work out at ground level, where we are lying dead in our trespasses and sins? Verse 5 of Thessalonians explains, first, that the gospel was preached. Second, God's power was doing its life-giving, quickening work, creating in us the capacity to hear the good news. God's Holy Spirit power brings to us what by nature we could never have – a vision of Jesus, the gift of repentance and an ability to believe. Third, conviction was created. God's Word came with 'deep conviction', convincing us of its truth and saving power.

So God's election, his choice of us, works outward, from the inner reality of his love to the outward preaching of the gospel: the exercise of the power of the Word of God, the energy of the Holy Spirit, producing conviction and giving the ability to repent and believe.

In the Bible, election (God's choice of us) is presented not as a theological conundrum to solve but as evidence of God's inexplicable love for us. Do you have any idea how loved you are? We know it in our heads, but sometimes the truth does not reach our hearts. Reassess your vision of God today – he is not distant and aloof from your suffering and anxiety; he is not a stern task-master waiting for you to make the grade. He is your heavenly Father, who gave you the precious gift of spiritual life simply because he loves you. He looked at you and said, 'I want you to be my son, I want you to be my daughter.' You are loved, you are valued, you are precious. Let the words roll around on your tongue and seep into the core of your being. Today, allow this truth to govern your emotions and shape your thoughts and actions.

Day 5

Read 1 Thessalonians 1:1–10
Key verses: 1 Thessalonians 1:6–8

....

⁶ You became imitators of us and of the Lord, for you welcomed the message in the midst of severe suffering with the joy given by the Holy Spirit. ⁷ And so you became a model to all the believers in Macedonia and Achaia. ⁸ The Lord's message rang out from you not only in Macedonia and Achaia – your faith in God has become known everywhere. Therefore we do not need to say anything about it.

Who are your role models? Who are the Christians you look to for inspiration and encouragement in the faith?

Here Paul promotes the Thessalonian church as a model. He does so not because the believers were perfect, but because of the priority they placed on the Word of God.

First, they received God's Word. Understanding and accepting the Bible message was core to their salvation and also tied them straight away into a system of imitation. In receiving the Word of God, they aligned themselves with the apostles, the men of the Word, and with the Lord Jesus, that great Man of the Word.

Second, they persevered in the Word. Despite the persecution, the Thessalonians continued to accept God's truth, believe his promises and trust his Son. We may not face the same type of persecution, but our faith will be tested to see if we hold on to God's Word in difficult times. Notice that the Thessalonians' perseverance was not a grim determination. The Holy Spirit gave them the spiritual joy of knowing the truth. And every time we open our Bibles, determined to persevere in the Word, the Spirit is ready to impart his own joy.

Third, they shared the Word: 'The Lord's message rang out from you not only in Macedonia and Achaia – your faith in God has become known everywhere.'

It was their focus on the Bible that made this church a model for others. The Word of God called it into existence, converted its members, and gave focus to its life and substance to its message.

What about your church? What about you? Are you a Bible person? Are you persevering in the Word of God? Are you sharing it with others?

On a scale of one to ten, rate the importance of the Bible in your life. Think about the influence it has on your decision-making; how you raise your family; how you plan for the future; and how you use your leisure time. Christians are called 'people of the Book', but is it really true? Is devotion to the Bible the distinguishing mark of your life? Don't wait any longer. Give the Bible back its rightful place: read it, study it, meditate on it. Allow it to transform you. Who knows, God could use your passion for his Word as a model for others.

Day 6

Read 1 Thessalonians 1:1–10
Key verses: 1 Thessalonians 1:9–10

....

⁹They themselves report what kind of reception you gave us. They tell how you turned to God from idols to serve the living and true God, ¹⁰and to wait for his Son from heaven, whom he raised from the dead – Jesus, who rescues us from the coming wrath.

Many Christians struggle with doubt. 'How can I be sure I'm really saved?' 'How can I know my sins are forgiven?' These questions plague us, stripping us of joy and peace, and hampering our service.

Of course, if it was down to us, and our abilities and reliability, then certainly our salvation would be in doubt. But our salvation is entirely dependent on that one single, blessed, central, all-sufficient person: our Lord Jesus Christ.

These verses remind us that Jesus' resurrection is the decisive proof that his work of salvation was effective.

God raising Jesus from the dead was heaven's confirmation sign that his work at Calvary was complete. Jesus' resurrection was the Father's 'Amen' to the Son's cry: 'It is finished.'

The consequences of Jesus' work on the cross continue. However, when Paul says, 'Jesus rescues us from the coming wrath', present tense, he doesn't mean that the work of salvation is still going on. Salvation was achieved once and for all on the cross. Jesus is not forever rescuing, he simply rescues for ever. So when Paul looks forward to that Day of Judgment and of standing before God, he has no fear. He has been rescued from the coming wrath. The same is true for us.

Some of us remember the exact moment when we 'turned to God'. The rest of us know we did; we just can't pinpoint the exact date and time of our conversion. But, whenever it happened, the important thing to remember is that when we 'turned to God', we entered into the finished work of salvation, and an eternal security in which we never need to fear God's wrath.

The devil is a grand master of doubt and lies – he's had years of practice! He whispers in your ear, 'If you were really saved, surely you wouldn't have done that?' and 'Could God really forgive that terrible sin?' Jesus' resurrection stands as a line in the sand, a marker for all of eternity, that the devil has been defeated and your sin has been paid for. Because of Christ's sacrifice, you are clothed in his righteousness and can look forward to that final day when you are welcomed into heaven. Bring your doubts, the sins that plague you and the failures of the past, and leave them at the foot of the cross. 'It is finished.' Rejoice in so great a salvation!

Day 7

Read 1 Thessalonians 2:1–16
Key verses: 1 Thessalonians 2:1–4

....

[1] You know, brothers and sisters, that our visit to you was not without results. [2] We had previously suffered and been treated outrageously in Philippi, as you know, but with the help of our God we dared to tell you his gospel in the face of strong opposition. [3] For the appeal we make does not spring from error or impure motives, nor are we trying to trick you. [4] On the contrary, we speak as those approved by God to be entrusted with the gospel. We are not trying to please people but God, who tests our hearts.

Every generation of Christians has to ask, 'How can we best share the gospel?' As culture, technology and resources change, what does effective evangelism look like? How can we share the gospel in ways that bear fruit in positive, unmistakable, lasting conversions?

Paul reminds the Thessalonian believers that his first visit to them was a fruitful time for the gospel, as people immediately turned to God. Why was this visit so successful? What was the reason for so many conversions? Paul gives two reasons. His first reason (we'll look at the second reason tomorrow) was the truth factor. He faithfully shared the gospel, which is the truth about and from God.

Twice in these four verses, Paul mentions the gospel. In verse 2 he talks of 'his gospel', which literally means 'the gospel of God'. Paul uses many parallel expressions. For example, he speaks of 'the gospel of his Son', by which he means that the Lord Jesus is the sum and substance of the gospel. He is the great subject of the gospel; he is its great content. Similarly, when elsewhere he speaks of 'the gospel of the grace of God', he means that the gospel message is a ministry of imparting the grace of God. But here by 'the gospel of God' he means origin and ownership. The gospel originated from God himself, and he is the owner and master of it.

Effective evangelism means us sharing the mighty gospel of God.

Have you ever found yourself in a conversation where, unexpectedly, you have the opportunity to share the gospel? Often when we are caught off guard, we don't know quite what to say. The temptation is to sugar-coat the gospel, to avoid talking about sin or judgment and to focus instead on the wonderful purposes God has for believers. Prepare for those conversations. What are the core components of the gospel? Practise presenting the gospel faithfully and gently. Research gospel resources that you would feel comfortable giving to your friends and colleagues. And most importantly, pray. Pray for opportunities to share the gospel and wisdom when those opportunities arise. If you don't already pray regularly for unbelievers to become Christians, choose five friends or family members, and commit to praying for them daily.

Day 8

Read 1 Thessalonians 2:1–16
Key verses: 1 Thessalonians 2:1–4

....

¹You know, brothers and sisters, that our visit to you was not without results. ²We had previously suffered and been treated outrageously in Philippi, as you know, but with the help of our God we dared to tell you his gospel in the face of strong opposition. ³For the appeal we make does not spring from error or impure motives, nor are we trying to trick you. ⁴On the contrary, we speak as those approved by God to be entrusted with the gospel. We are not trying to please people but God, who tests our hearts.

Many of the people we rub shoulders with will never darken the door of a church. They will never listen to a sermon. However, they are still watching to see if our 'walk' matches our 'talk'.

Look again at verses 1–4. Paul brought the truth of the gospel to the Thessalonians with a holy and dedicated life, and a heart approved by God. Effective evangelism has never been about simply saying the right words or knowing the right facts. God entrusts the gospel to those whose lives he has tested and approved. What exactly is God looking for? Or, more precisely, whom is God looking for?

Those who consciously rely on God's strength. The freedom and courage that Paul and his friends experienced as they shared the gospel was not human stoicism, nor was it making light of their suffering; it was a conscious reliance on 'the help of our God'.

Those who present the good news simply. 'Tell you the gospel' in verse 2 literally means 'chatting' the gospel.

Those who are not concerned about themselves. Paul faced 'strong opposition', which refers to the danger and threats in Philippi, and also to the hesitations within his own heart. However, he was prepared to accept the risks and live with the hesitation.

Those who have integrity. Paul had integrity of mind, emotion and will. His conscience was clear because he told the truth about the gospel and he did not use deceitful methods.

Those who desire to please God. If Paul had not been flogged in Philippi, he would not have known whether he was promoting the gospel for his own purposes, or out of a desire solely to please God. His willingness to suffer revealed his true motives and that he was 'approved by God to be entrusted with the gospel'.

Do you share these defining traits? Could God entrust you with his gospel?

The gospel is never delivered in a vacuum; it comes wrapped up in our personalities. Our lives are adverts for the gospel. Take time to pray through these traits. Ask God to highlight the areas where you need to change and ask for his Holy Spirit help. And do not despise your suffering – who knows whether the suffering that you have just passed through, or are passing through, or which will start today or tomorrow, may be God approving you to be entrusted with the gospel. Accept his discipline, hold on to him, love him with a pure heart, live out the gospel and pray intentionally for opportunities to share Christ with others.

Day 9

Read 1 Thessalonians 2:1–16
Key verses: 1 Thessalonians 2:5–9

....

> [5] *You know we never used flattery, nor did we put on a mask to cover up greed – God is our witness.* [6] *We were not looking for praise from people, not from you or anyone else, even though as apostles of Christ we could have asserted our authority.* [7] *Instead, we were like young children among you.*
>
> *Just as a nursing mother cares for her children,* [8] *so we cared for you. Because we loved you so much, we were delighted to share with you not only the gospel of God but our lives as well.* [9] *Surely you remember, brothers and sisters, our toil and hardship; we worked night and day in order not to be a burden to anyone while we preached the gospel of God to you.*

Evangelism is not meant to be a guilt-inducing add-on extra in our already busy lives. Each of us has work colleagues, family, a circle of friends – people we already have relationships with, but who do not yet know Jesus. Paul urges us to invest our lives into these people, and he gives us an illustration of how to do it: a nursing mother.

Perhaps a better translation of verse 7 would be: 'Just as a nurse-mother cherishes her very own children, so we cherished you.' A mother will certainly cherish her children. But a nurse is trained, and here she is looking after her own children. Paul says that if you are going to be evangelists, you have got to demonstrate these qualities of tenderness, love and care. Essentially un-self-seeking devotion is vital.

What did this look like in practice? Well, in verses 5–6, Paul explains how he shunned self-advantage: he didn't try to cajole people with clever words; he didn't need to cover up any greed; he didn't expect to be praised or put on a pedestal. Instead, he pursued what was to the Thessalonians' advantage: he worked tirelessly so they wouldn't need to give him financial support and so the gospel would be free to them. He sums it up: 'We loved you so much, we were delighted to share with you not only the gospel of God but our lives as well.'

What a picture for us to copy!

Think about the five individuals mentioned on day 7. How could you be a nurse-mother to them? How could you demonstrate self-sacrificing love and care and work for their advantage? Pray through your day and all the specific opportunities you have to 'share life' with these people. If your plans go awry today and people interrupt your schedule, see this as God giving you an extra opportunity to show self-sacrificing love! Meditate on the self-giving of Christ as your motivation today.

Day 10

Read 1 Thessalonians 2:1–16
Key verses: 1 Thessalonians 2:10–12

....

[10] You are witnesses, and so is God, of how holy, righteous and blameless we were among you who believed. [11] For you know that we dealt with each of you as a father deals with his own children, [12] encouraging, comforting and urging you to live lives worthy of God, who calls you into his kingdom and glory.

As we chat about the gospel in our workplaces, colleges, homes and the ordinary routines of daily life, Paul gives us another picture. Whereas the illustration of the mother emphasized self-sacrificing devotion, the illustration of the father highlights holy living and encouraging teaching. Paul was like a mother and a father to the Thessalonians as he shared the gospel with them. He urges us to follow his example and to:

Be a role model. Paul modelled holiness to the Thessalonians – 'You are witnesses . . . of how holy, righteous and blameless we were among you' (verse 10).

Guide in the right direction. In verse 12, Paul both encourages and exhorts the Thessalonians. Like a father, he gave positive encouragement to guide them in the right direction and was there to comfort them when they failed. But all the time, undergirding the encouragement and comfort, his purpose was to share the truth with them.

Remind them of God. Like a father, Paul reminded the Thessalonians 'to live lives worthy of God' (verse 12). He reminded them of the sufficiency of God and the obedience their great King deserved. He also urged them to persevere in their faith, reminding them of the future glory awaiting them.

You might not like the idea, but people are watching you. Your children, work colleagues, college friends, parents at the school gate, people in your home group or book group – they are all watching you. They are taking notice of whether your actions and conversations match your beliefs. They are looking to see whether your faith really is authentic and makes a difference to your life. Pray that you will model Christ well today.

Pray that instead of consisting of gossip or trivia, your conversations will point people to the way of truth and encourage them to press on in the faith, looking forward to heaven.

Day 11

Read 1 Thessalonians 2:1–16
Key verses: 1 Thessalonians 2:13–14

....

> [13] *And we also thank God continually because, when you received the word of God, which you heard from us, you accepted it not as a human word, but as it actually is, the word of God, which is indeed at work in you who believe.* [14] *For you, brothers and sisters, became imitators of God's churches in Judea, which are in Christ Jesus: you suffered from your own people the same things those churches suffered from the Jews.*

Today, many of us have multiple copies of the Bible, in various translations, and on numerous electronic devices. It is easy to become complacent about the fact that the Bible is actually divine truth. Although they were brought to us through human agents, the pages we read are the very words of God in the fullest sense. So how should we respond to the Bible? How did the Thessalonians respond?

They 'received' it (verse 13). The Thessalonians recognized it was authoritative.

They 'accepted' it (verse 13). More than just recognizing the authority of the Word of God, they opened their minds and hearts to it and welcomed it as something lovely.

They 'believed' it. The Word was 'at work in you who believe' (verse 13). They believed the Bible's teaching and promises, and then, in faithful obedience, acted upon its commands.

They 'suffered' (verse 14). Paul has already spoken about this in 1 Thessalonians 1:6. As before, it is not the form of the testing that matters, but its inevitability. Their reception of the Word was tested by the onset of persecution. The Word of God is always challenged. Part of our true reception of the Word is not only to receive it as authoritative, to welcome it as lovely, to believe and obey it, but to persevere in its truth in the face of any odds.

Do you recognize yourself in Paul's description of the Thessalonians? Have you received God's Word? Have you accepted it, believed it and suffered for it? What is holding you back from fully trusting the divine Word of God? Is there a promise you need to hold on to, a command you need to obey, or a circumstance you need to persevere in? Meditate on these verses from Psalm 119. Pray that God would increase your love and devotion to his Word, so you could say with the psalmist:

- 'You are my portion, LORD;
  I have promised to obey your words' (verse 57).

- 'How sweet are your words to my taste,
  sweeter than honey to my mouth!' (verse 103).

- 'Your word is a lamp for my feet,
  a light on my path' (verse 105).

- 'Your statutes are my heritage for ever;
  they are the joy of my heart' (verse 111).

- 'You are my refuge and my shield;
  I have put my hope in your word' (verse 114).

- 'Your promises have been thoroughly tested,
  and your servant loves them' (verse 140).

Day 12

Read 1 Thessalonians 2:1–16
Key verses: 1 Thessalonians 2:14–16

....

[14] You suffered from your own people the same things those churches suffered from the Jews [15] who killed the Lord Jesus and the prophets and also drove us out. They displease God and are hostile to everyone [16] in their effort to keep us from speaking to the Gentiles so that they may be saved. In this way they always heap up their sins to the limit. The wrath of God has come upon them at last.

The gospel is only 'good news' if you accept it.

These verses are about those who reject the Word of God. Paul explains that the Jews 'killed the Lord Jesus and the prophets and also drove us out'. Essentially, they had the Word of God in the loveliest personal form of Jesus; they had the Word of God in the inspired form of scriptural prophecy; they had the Word of God in its up-to-date form of New Testament apostleship – and they rejected it out of hand. They also rejected the Word of God's evangelistic benefit for the world: 'They . . . are hostile to everyone in their effort to keep us away from speaking to the Gentiles so that they may be saved.'

Paul is not being anti-Semitic. But he's saying that where there is refusal of Jesus, a rejection of the prophets, a driving out of the apostles and a barring of the evangelistic message – where there is that fourfold rejection of the Word of God, there cannot be anything else but the utmost judgment of God.

This is no polemic, simply a basic statement of a dreadful but inescapable fact: that when people reject the Word of God, they come under judgment in its full and final form.

The judgment of God is a sobering thought. Pray for an openness to the gospel in the various ministries your church is involved in: the Sunday school, toddler group, ministry among the older folk and the youth. Think of the times you will hear God's Word today: in the music playing on your headphones, the sermon you downloaded to listen to as you travel, the devotional time you have with your family, the Bible study you will join this evening. Pray that in each of those instances, you will accept God's Word as his message to you, whether that is a rebuke, challenge, encouragement or comfort. As Paul exhorts us in Colossians 3:16: 'Let the message of Christ dwell among you richly.'

Day 13

Read 1 Thessalonians 2:17 – 4:8
Key verses: 1 Thessalonians 2:17–20

....

17 But, brothers and sisters, when we were orphaned by being separated from you for a short time (in person, not in thought), out of our intense longing we made every effort to see you. 18 For we wanted to come to you – certainly I, Paul, did, again and again – but Satan blocked our way. 19 For what is our hope, our joy, or the crown in which we will glory in the presence of our Lord Jesus when he comes? Is it not you? 20 Indeed, you are our glory and joy.

How would you describe your relationship with the other people in your church, home group, those you serve alongside on the rota?

Paul describes his separation from the Thessalonians using a very strong image, of 'orphaned' children. He has already described his relationship with them as like that of a nurse-mother and a caring, directive, loving father. He also frequently addresses these believers as 'brothers and sisters'. In fact, he uses the term 'brothers' more frequently in his letters to the Thessalonians than when he writes to any other church. He is a mother to them, he is a father to them, he is a brother among brothers, and now he is a child bereaved of its parents. How greatly Paul loved these Thessalonian Christians!

This is no formal or pretend relationship. He describes himself being snatched away, bereaved, for a short time, 'in person, not in thought'. His heart is engaged in this relationship. He longs for them with an 'intense longing'. Indeed, he says in verse 19 that the prospect of the coming of the Lord Jesus itself would be less a matter of hope, joy and glory if Paul thought they were not going to be there ready.

How deeply, how affectionately, how from the heart Paul loves these Thessalonians.

We talk about church being a family. And most of the time we rub along like a family, albeit a rather dysfunctional one! But one sharp word, a minor disagreement, and we quickly forget about our family ties in favour of factions and cliques. Pray for your own church, that there will be unity, love and understanding among you. Pray that you will play your part by avoiding gossip, forgiving, encouraging and, where necessary, building bridges and seeking peace. Look for an opportunity to show love and care to someone from your church today.

Day 14

Read 1 Thessalonians 2:17 – 4:8
Key verses: 1 Thessalonians 2:17–20

• •

[17] But, brothers and sisters, when we were orphaned by being separated from you for a short time (in person, not in thought), out of our intense longing we made every effort to see you. [18] For we wanted to come to you – certainly I, Paul, did, again and again – but Satan blocked our way. [19] For what is our hope, our joy, or the crown in which we will glory in the presence of our Lord Jesus when he comes? Is it not you? [20] Indeed, you are our glory and joy.

Are you giving Satan too much or too little credit for what's going on in your life?

Today we are looking again at verses 17–20 because we need to get Satan's power into perspective. Satan is mentioned by name only nine times in Paul's letters. Compare that with the hundreds of times that Paul refers to Jesus. In the Bible, Satan does not operate as a free agent, but only within the sovereign purposes of God. The story of Job, for example, reminds us that Satan can only operate within the permission, direction and limitation of God (see also Revelation 20).

Isaiah describes the way God runs history as like a horse (Isaiah 63:13–14) and its rider. The horse has the energy to jump a fence, but will not get over it unless the rider directs him to it. In this picture, Satan is the horse and on his back is the great divine rider, directing all that sinful power and energy to perform holy purposes. Satan always has the Lord on his back!

So we need to get Satan's power into proportion. There is a supernatural power raging against us. There is ceaseless malevolence, the god of this world, who prevented Paul reaching Thessalonica. But isn't it marvellous that Paul couldn't get back? As a result, he and his companions had a much better and richer experience. They learnt that, apostle or no apostle, ministry or no ministry, God was looking after his church.

We can begin to see why the Lord directed Satan to put up the roadblock: so that Paul could learn, so that the Thessalonians could learn, so that we could learn that our spiritual welfare rests in the hands of God.

As you reflect on the frustrations, sadness and suffering that have marked your life, do not be dismayed or despondent. Satan is not some wild horse riding roughshod over your life, going where he wants, doing what he chooses. Yes, imagine Satan as a horse, but with God as the divine rider, permitting, limiting and determining every step. To the untrained eye it might look as if Satan is winning a victory. But, as Paul and countless others would testify, God will use even Satan's actions to accomplish his purpose in your life. Cling on to God's sovereignty and his good purposes today.

Day 15

Read 1 Thessalonians 2:17 – 4:8

Key verses: 1 Thessalonians 3:1–5

....

¹So when we could stand it no longer, we thought it best to be left by ourselves in Athens. ²We sent Timothy, who is our brother and co-worker in God's service in spreading the gospel of Christ, to strengthen and encourage you in your faith, ³so that no one would be unsettled by these trials. For you know quite well that we are destined for them. ⁴In fact, when we were with you, we kept telling you that we would be persecuted. And it turned out that way, as you well know. ⁵For this reason, when I could stand it no longer, I sent to find out about your faith. I was afraid that in some way the tempter had tempted you and that our labours might have been in vain.

Have you ever asked God, 'Why?' 'Why am I suffering like this?' 'Why is the person I love suffering like this?'

The 'trials' (verse 3) that we face may be persecution, they may be the ordinary troubles and difficulties of life, but Paul knows that they often 'unsettle' believers. With troubles come doubt and a shaking of faith, and the pressure of Satan to lever us away from firm and believing attachment to the Lord Jesus Christ.

Paul had explained that suffering was what 'we are destined for', but we, like the Thessalonians, don't want to believe it. James says, 'Consider it pure joy, my brothers and sisters, whenever you face trials of many kinds' (James 1:2). But we don't listen to him; we don't consider it joy. Peter says, 'Do not be surprised at the fiery ordeal that has come on you to test you' (1 Peter 4:12). We don't believe him either; we think it very strange indeed. And we go on with our 'Why? Why?' and our doubting of the goodness of God.

But Paul says not to let Satan tempt us when trials come. Grasp today, and hold from today the fact that this is not strange, but an inevitability. It is part of our discipleship, it is what we were 'destined' for (verse 3; see also Acts 14:22).

When Paul wrote to the Philippians he said, 'You know my imprisonment, contrary to what you might have expected, is becoming a real testimony to the gospel, because they know that I am in prison for Christ – I am on duty for the gospel' (Philippians 1:12–13, paraphrased). It is the same word 'destined' here. Suffering is where we are on duty for God; it is the appointed sphere of our discipleship. It is what we were 'destined' for. So the real question should not be 'Why?' but 'What?' 'What should I do in this situation to grow in my discipleship, to demonstrate my devotion to Christ?'

When I was going through a particular trial, a friend wisely said to me, 'You will never pass this way again. Make sure there is something in it for him.'

Read Psalm 23. Why does God sometimes lead us by green pastures and quiet waters? Why is our portion sometimes the dark valley? What comes between the two in Psalm 23? 'He guides me along the right paths for his name's sake' (verse 3). What is the right path? It is a path that makes proper sense to God. We think the only proper path is the one that makes sense to us, and when suffering comes, we say, 'It doesn't make sense.' Yes, it does. It makes sense to him. That's all that matters. Trust in the sovereign hand of God today and remember: 'You will never pass this way again. Make sure there is something in it for him.'

Day 16

Read 1 Thessalonians 2:17 – 4:8
Key verses: 1 Thessalonians 3:6–10

∙∙∙

⁶But Timothy has just now come to us from you and has brought good news about your faith and love. He has told us that you always have pleasant memories of us and that you long to see us, just as we also long to see you. ⁷Therefore, brothers and sisters, in all our distress and persecution we were encouraged about you because of your faith. ⁸For now we really live, since you are standing firm in the Lord. ⁹How can we thank God enough for you in return for all the joy we have in the presence of our God because of you? ¹⁰Night and day we pray most earnestly that we may see you again and supply what is lacking in your faith.

What do you think a 'successful' Christian life looks like? How would you describe a 'victorious' Christian life?

If we imagine that Christian victory means never again being tempted by Satan, we will quickly become disillusioned. Likewise, if we imagine being a Christian means experiencing heaven on earth, no more trials or suffering, we will be sorely disappointed.

Paul doesn't say to the Thessalonians, 'What a mighty victory you have scored in driving Satan out and drastically changing your circumstances in answer to prayer.' That is not the essence of earthly victory. And yet they scored a triumph. Paul describes it as just as good news as the gospel, a fresh injection of life for which he didn't know how to thank God enough.

So what was their victory? It was Christian stability: 'now we really live, since you are standing firm in the Lord' (verse 8). And it was also Christian virtue, as shown in verse 6: 'Timothy . . . has brought good news about your faith and love.' Paul has already mentioned their faith, love and stability in 1:3. For him, Christian victory was not in the drama, but in faith, love and stickability in the ordinary realities of life.

Despite your prayers, your circumstances may not change, and you may still feel Satan prowling round you like a hungry lion. Don't be discouraged. God never promised us heaven on earth; trials and suffering are part of his plan. Pray for yourself and your loved ones who are going through difficult times, that you will stand firm in the Lord, demonstrating faith and love. Some days, holding on to God is all we can do, but it is all we need to do! God is not looking for dramatic displays of devotion, but faithfulness in the everyday ordinariness of life. Meditate today on Paul's outrageous criteria for victorious Christian living: 'We remember before our God and Father your work produced by faith, your labour prompted by love, and your endurance inspired by hope in our Lord Jesus Christ' (1 Thessalonians 1:3).

Day 17

Read 1 Thessalonians 2:17 – 4:8
Key verses: 1 Thessalonians 3:11–13

....

11 Now may our God and Father himself and our Lord Jesus clear the way for us to come to you. 12 May the Lord make your love increase and overflow for each other and for everyone else, just as ours does for you. 13 May he strengthen your hearts so that you will be blameless and holy in the presence of our God and Father when our Lord Jesus comes with all his holy ones.

How would you describe your prayer life? Our prayers are often a good indicator of the state of our relationship with God and a mirror to our own soul. Can you see how Paul's focus shifted during the course of his prayer? Do you need to follow his example?

In verse 10 Paul prayed, 'Night and day we pray most earnestly that we may see you again and supply what is lacking in your faith.' Paul had felt that the Thessalonians' spiritual welfare was largely dependent on him being there to minister to them. He was anxious that without his care and guidance, Satan would be gaining ground. But then Timothy reported back that the Thessalonians were getting on fine in Paul's absence.

Paul then returns to prayer with a completely different attitude, leaving it entirely to God whether he ever gets back to see them or not. He prays, 'Now may our God and Father himself and our Lord Jesus clear the way for us to come to you' (verse 11) – but whether he gets there or not, what does it matter? Paul realizes that God is looking after his people. It is the Lord who will cause their love for one another to increase and their hearts to be strengthened. The welfare of the church rests in the hands of a sovereign and loving God.

This realization shifts the focus of Paul's prayer, from verse 10 to verses 11–12. It is as if he is saying, 'If the Lord brings me back, great! But if he doesn't, he is there and he will make you perfect in holiness, and he will make your faith and your love go on increasing and out-reaching. You are all right. You are in the hands of God, and I'm happy to leave you there.'

It is easy to develop a messiah complex, assuming that events or circumstances depend solely on our organization and active participation. But the lesson Paul learnt is one we need to grasp – God is in control, not us! It is not up to us to orchestrate our children's lives, our parents' lives or our spouse's life. Entrusting our loved ones into God's hands shouldn't be a last resort, but a first port of call. Name the loved ones who are on your mind. Picture them in the hands of God. Pray Psalm 121 for them.

I lift up my eyes to the mountains –
    where does my help come from?
My help comes from the LORD,
    the Maker of heaven and earth.

He will not let your foot slip –
    he who watches over you will not slumber;
indeed, he who watches over Israel
    will neither slumber nor sleep.

The LORD watches over you –
    the LORD is your shade at your right hand;
the sun will not harm you by day,
    nor the moon by night.

The LORD will keep you from all harm –
    he will watch over your life;
the LORD will watch over your coming and going
    both now and for evermore.

Day 18

Read 1 Thessalonians 2:17 – 4:8
Key verses: 1 Thessalonians 4:1–8

....

¹As for other matters, brothers and sisters, we instructed you how to live in order to please God, as in fact you are living. Now we ask you and urge you in the Lord Jesus to do this more and more. ²For you know what instructions we gave you by the authority of the Lord Jesus.

³It is God's will that you should be sanctified: that you should avoid sexual immorality; ⁴that each of you should learn to control your own body in a way that is holy and honourable, ⁵not in passionate lust like the pagans, who do not know God; ⁶and that in this matter no one should wrong or take advantage of a brother or sister. The Lord will punish all those who commit such sins, as we told you and warned you before. ⁷For God did not call us to be impure, but to live a holy life. ⁸Therefore, anyone who rejects this instruction does not reject a human being but God, the very God who gives you his Holy Spirit.

Are you growing in holiness? Just as physical growth signals health, so does spiritual growth.

Paul is urging the Thessalonians to press on in the matter of holiness. And his plea is as follows:

Keep obeying God. Paul had given the Thessalonians instructions and they were to keep on obeying these commands from God. Obedience to God is how we pursue holiness.

Keep knowing God. The Thessalonians were clearly struggling with sexual morality. Paul's answer to their temptation was to 'know God'. If we are plagued with lapses into sexual sin, then the key is to be an informed believer, continually striving to get to know God better.

Keep fearing God. God will punish those who sin; he is the avenger. A healthy fear of God keeps us on the track of holiness.

Keep trusting God. Verse 7 reminds us that God called us not to an impure life, but to holiness. Holiness is not an external objective, rather the reality to which we have been brought. God has called us into the context of holiness and we have got to learn to become what we are. So we say to God, 'I am desperately unholy in all my inclinations; I desperately want to be holy. I believe that you have given me all that I need to be holy, therefore it is worth all the striving and struggling.'

Keep relying on the Holy Spirit. God's Spirit within us is called the Holy Spirit because it is his task to administer holiness to us, as we walk with God. God forever keeps on giving us his Spirit and we live a holy life when we enjoy, respect and draw upon that Spirit.

How would you rate your growth in holiness? Have you grown in holiness in the past week, past month or year? Think through Paul's recipe for holiness.

- Is there a particular area of your life where God is asking you to obey him?

- What measures are you taking to know God better? What are your devotional times like? How is your prayer life?

- Do you have an appropriate fear of God? Does fear of disobeying God keep you faithful?

- Is there something you need to trust God for?

- Are you relying on the Holy Spirit or are you trying to please God in your own strength?

You started the journey of faith well, so don't give up now. Keep pressing on! God has given you all the means to grow in holiness, so ask for his strength and help today.

Day 19

Read 1 Thessalonians 4:9–18
Key verses: 1 Thessalonians 4:9–10

....

9Now about your love for one another we do not need to write to you, for you yourselves have been taught by God to love each other. 10And in fact, you do love all of God's family throughout Macedonia. Yet we urge you, brothers and sisters, to do so more and more.

Is your church worth joining? Have you created an atmosphere of Christian love which attracts outsiders as you share the gospel with them?

Paul believed that it was only from a strong base of love that the church could reach out to the world. He knows that the Thessalonians already love one another, but he urges them to do so more and more because brotherly love is such a foundational principle for the church.

He explains that they have been 'taught by God to love each other'. When the Thessalonians became Christians, God shared his mind with them, so Christian intuition began to govern their relationships. But more than that, Paul had taught them about loving one another from Scripture. Our intuition to love must be confirmed, strengthened, directed and controlled by the teaching of the Word of God.

Love within the church is not a requirement that can be set on the side; it is for now. It is not a requirement that can be exhausted. It is something that must always be on the increase, an immediate and endless obligation for the people of God.

We are never too old, too far along in the faith or too busy to be reminded about the need for love. If there is no love in the church, then we have nothing to offer the world. It is costly to love – it takes time and energy, and it interferes with our personal plans – but it is non-negotiable. Meditate on Jesus' words in John 13:34–35.

A new command I give you: love one another. As I have loved you, so you must love one another. By this everyone will know that you are my disciples, if you love one another.

Consider Christ's love for you. How does that define the type of love you should have for others in your church? What difference will loving like this make?

Day 20

Read 1 Thessalonians 4:9–18
Key verses: 1 Thessalonians 4:11–12

....

11 Make it your ambition to lead a quiet life: you should mind your own business and work with your hands, just as we told you, 12 so that your daily life may win the respect of outsiders and so that you will not be dependent on anybody.

Think about your own church and the occasions where there has been strife or division.

Paul suggests that brotherly love breaks down because of frenzied activity, undue interference in people's lives and trading on the goodwill of others. So he urges the Thessalonians to safeguard their love by the following:

Lead a quiet life. Paul is talking about tranquillity of temperament rather than circumstances. Be a tranquil person, be amenable.

Mind your own business. Look after your own needs.

Work with your hands. Earn your own living.

If you live like this, first, it will impact your evangelism. The world will notice and respect a church where these qualities exist. Second, you will not 'be dependent on anybody' and 'you will not have any need'. This seems a strange phrase, but the background is Acts 2 – 4, when no one had any needs because no one considered their possessions their own, and distribution was made to anyone who had need.

So, if we are tranquil in temperament, if we mind our own business and earn our own living, the world will sit up and take notice, and we will be in a position to cultivate and cherish and support a loving fellowship.

What is your ambition? What is the passion or driving force in your life? Not many of us would say our primary ambition was to love our church family! But accept Paul's challenge. Make it your goal this week to love the people in your church. This may mean working on your temperament, not being nosy and interfering unnecessarily in people's lives, or working hard to support yourself rather than expecting others to bail you out.

With Paul's words in front of you, ask yourself: 'Am I increasing the love quota in my church or am I a drain? Is my behaviour likely to attract people to church or put them off?' Invite the Holy Spirit to convict, challenge and encourage you. Allow him to search your heart and reshape your ambitions.

Day 21

Read 1 Thessalonians 4:13–18
Key verses: 1 Thessalonians 4:13–14

....

13 Brothers and sisters, we do not want you to be uninformed about those who sleep in death, so that you do not grieve like the rest of mankind, who have no hope. 14 For we believe that Jesus died and rose again, and so we believe that God will bring with Jesus those who have fallen asleep in him.

Death is one of the few certainties of life.

Paul, full of pastoral concern, wanted the Thessalonians to be well informed. They were anxious that fellow believers who had died would miss the second coming. So Paul allays their fears and reminds them, and us, that we can face the sorrows of life and look forward to the glories of heaven because we know that:

Death has been transformed. For us, death is the impenetrable and irreversible reality, but for Jesus it is the sleep from which he will shake us awake. Just like he did with Jairus' daughter in Mark 5.

Grief has been transformed. How is our grief different from those who do not know Christ? Surprisingly perhaps, our grief is sharper. We feel grief more keenly because our emotions have been sharpened by the regenerating work of the Holy Spirit. Our grief is also different because it is in the context of eternal hope; while we grieve, we also have the glorious expectation of a joyful reunion.

Hope has been transformed. The Christian hope is sure and certain because it is based on Jesus' finished work. When he died and rose again we were associated with that death and resurrection, so that we both died and rose with him. So after our death we have the sure hope that there will be resurrection and transformation.

As Christians, we are not immune from sorrow. We will face the death of loved ones just like our non-Christian neighbours. And, like Jesus weeping at Lazarus' tomb, we will feel that grief keenly. But Jesus' death and resurrection means that more than anything else, our mourning is transformed. We grieve only for a short time, knowing that one day soon those who are asleep in Christ will rise to meet him in the air. If you are mourning today, allow these truths to penetrate your grief. If you are supporting those who grieve, encourage them with these words. With gentleness, lift their eyes to the horizon to watch expectantly for the imminent return of Christ – our sure and certain hope. As Paul says, 'Listen, I tell you a mystery: we will not all sleep, but we will all be changed – in a flash, in the twinkling of an eye, at the last trumpet. For the trumpet will sound, the dead will be raised imperishable, and we will be changed' (1 Corinthians 15:51–52).

Day 22

Read 1 Thessalonians 4:13–18
Key verses: 1 Thessalonians 4:13–14

....

13 Brothers and sisters, we do not want you to be uninformed about those who sleep in death, so that you do not grieve like the rest of mankind, who have no hope. 14 For we believe that Jesus died and rose again, and so we believe that God will bring with Jesus those who have fallen asleep in him.

Woody Allen famously said, 'I'm not afraid of death, I just don't want to be there when it happens.'

While we may not fear death, many of us fear the process of dying. We are anxious about the pain, the loss of control and the dependence on others. But Paul's words speak comfort to our hearts.

Verse 14 literally refers to those who have fallen asleep not 'in' but 'through' Jesus. This means that our death is stage-managed by him, that the circumstances of our dying have been organized by his sovereign hand and that the timing of our death has been decided in heaven. It is all through Jesus. Through him we go to be with him. And going to be with him, we have a guarantee that we who have died before he comes will nonetheless share in his coming, because God will bring with him those who sleep through Jesus. If that should be his portion for us, we will not miss out on any of the glory of the second coming. We might even have a better view of it! We will come with him, having been with him.

Take comfort and strength from the promise that God is sovereign and even your death will be stage-managed by him. In the meantime, learn submission, patience and dependence on God. Then, when the final act comes, you will be ready to play your part with humility and obedience.

Meditate on Dietrich Bonhoeffer's words:

Death is only dreadful for those who live in dread and fear of it. Death is not wild and terrible, if only we can be still and hold fast to God's Word. Death is not bitter, if we have not become bitter ourselves. Death is grace, the greatest gift of grace that God gives to people who believe in him. Death is mild, death is sweet and gentle;

it beckons to us with heavenly power, if only we realize that it is the gateway to our homeland, the tabernacle of joy, the everlasting kingdom of peace.

How do we know that dying is so dreadful? Who knows whether, in our human fear and anguish we are only shivering and shuddering at the most glorious, heavenly, blessed event in the world? Death is hell and night and cold, if it is not transformed by our faith. But that is just what is so marvelous, that we can transform death.

Eric Metaxas, *Bonhoeffer: Pastor, Martyr, Prophet, Spy* (Thomas Nelson, 2011), p. 531.

Day 23

Read 1 Thessalonians 4:13–18
Key verse: 1 Thessalonians 4:16

••

16 For the Lord himself will come down from heaven, with a loud command, with the voice of the archangel and with the trumpet call of God, and the dead in Christ will rise first.

Have you ever wondered what the return of Christ will be like?

We do not know many details, but one is guaranteed: his second coming will be very different from his first. Christ's return will be heralded with a loud command, presumably from God the Father, for who else knows when Christ is going to return and who else has the authority to give this command? The archangel Michael, the leader of the angel armies, will announce Christ's victory (see Jude 9; Daniel 10:13, 21; 12:1; Revelation 12:7). And then the trumpet will sound. Why will there be a trumpet?

- It is the trumpet of Exodus 19:16 which signals 'God is here'.

- It is the trumpet of Joel 2:1 which signals the great and awesome day of the Lord has at last come.

- It is the trumpet of Jubilee in Leviticus 25:9 announcing the release of slaves and the remission of debts.

- It is the trumpet of Isaiah 27:12–13 which sounds so that the people of God scattered in Egypt and Assyria may be brought home to Zion.

- It is the trumpet of Matthew 24:31 where the angels of God gather the elect from the four corners of the earth.

The trumpet of God will gather his elect from past, present and future, and from north, south, east and west.

Are you looking forward to that day?

I remember as a child wanting Christ to return, but hoping that he would wait until after Christmas! Even as adults we can get so caught up in the good things of life – family, friendships, celebrations, work, holidays – that Jesus' return is not a top priority. We talk about it, but we don't yearn for it.

Close your eyes and imagine the scene. Jesus Christ himself coming down to walk on earth, the skies shuddering as God the Father gives the command and the archangel announces his victory. The trumpet blasts gathering all the family of God to their heavenly home. The glory and majesty of Christ will be unmistakable – every eye will see it.

Pray that as you go through today, Christ's return will shape your behaviour, attitudes and thoughts: 'You ought to live holy and godly lives as you look forward to the day of God and speed its coming' (2 Peter 3:11–12).

Day 24

Read 1 Thessalonians 4:13–18
Key verses: 1 Thessalonians 4:16–17

....

16 For the Lord himself will come down from heaven, with a loud command, with the voice of the archangel and with the trumpet call of God, and the dead in Christ will rise first. 17 After that, we who are still alive and are left will be caught up together with them in the clouds to meet the Lord in the air. And so we will be with the Lord for ever.

What will happen to us at the second coming?

Paul explains that the bodies of those who have died will be raised to meet their souls, which once left them, and there will be a mighty reconstitution of a total redeemed humanity. But what about us who remain? Paul says, 'We who are still alive and are left will be caught up together with them in the clouds to meet the Lord in the air.'

There is obviously symbolism here. In the Bible, the clouds are the presence of God. After the exodus, God lived among the people in a cloudy, fiery pillar. The cloud said, 'God is here.' When Jesus, Peter, James and John stood on the Mount of Transfiguration, the cloud over-shadowed them; and out of the cloud came the voice that said, 'This is my Son: God is here.' And we are caught up in the clouds, into the very presence of God. The air is the usurped dominion of Satan, the prince of the power of the air (Ephesians 2:2). But we will enter into his usurped dominion because he is gone for ever. Only Jesus reigns.

The symbolism is important – with Jesus we will be caught into the presence of God; we will enter into his eternal triumph. But there is also objectivity and reality: we will be caught up. The phrase literally is 'we will be snatched' from the earth. And if we are alive on that day, we will be lifted bodily into heaven and stand before Jesus in the fullness of redemption. We will meet him in the clouds in the air.

Therefore encourage one another with these words.
(1 Thessalonians 4:18)

Paul wrote these verses not to satisfy our curiosity or to give us a timeline for future events. These verses are to spur us on, to encourage us in the faith. So tell yourself these words; speak them to your own heart.

If you are:

• struggling with health or family issues

• facing unemployment

• battling mental illness

• grieving

• celebrating success at work or in your family

• living with financial hardship or poverty

• caught up in the mundane routines of life . . .

Remember: 'We . . . will be caught up . . . in the clouds to meet the Lord in the air. And so we will be with the Lord for ever.'

Today, in your conversations with other believers, 'encourage them with these words'.

Day 25

Read 1 Thessalonians 5:1–11
Key verses: 1 Thessalonians 5:1–5

....

¹Now, brothers and sisters, about times and dates we do not need to write to you ²for you know very well that the day of the Lord will come like a thief in the night. ³While people are saying, 'Peace and safety', destruction will come on them suddenly, as labour pains on a pregnant woman, and they will not escape.

⁴But you, brothers and sisters, are not in darkness so that this day should surprise you like a thief. ⁵You are all children of the light and children of the day. We do not belong to the night or to the darkness.

Many people mock the idea of God's judgment. They don't believe it will ever come; they think that God is too nice to mete out judgment or they are too good to deserve it.

For those who complacently believe that life will always go on as it has done, and that their past will never catch up with them, Christ's return spells disaster. Paul makes it clear that although we cannot put a date on Christ's return, like a thief it will come unexpectedly and, like labour pains, it will be inescapable.

However, believers do not need to fear Christ's return because:

We are not in darkness. Darkness means ignorance, estrangement from God (Ephesians 4:18). We no longer live in darkness; we live in a new setting, a new environment. As Paul reminds us in Colossians 1:12–13, '[Give] joyful thanks to the Father, who has qualified you to share in the inheritance of his holy people in the kingdom of light. For he has rescued us from the dominion of darkness and brought us into the kingdom of the Son he loves.'

We are children of the light, children of the day. As well as a new setting we have been given a new nature, one with new powers of behaviour built in, but also the characteristic lifestyle that goes with daytime.

We are not of the night. We owe it nothing; it cannot command our loyalty. We have been brought into a new setting, we have been given a new nature, and we have been called to a new commitment. We live already, in our essential Christian nature, in that day into which he will usher us at his second coming. The day is coming; but, in reality, that day has dawned because already we are living in the light, with a new nature, new powers of behaviour and a new allegiance to the Lord Jesus Christ. And when the day comes, all that we have now as potential and enjoy in part will come into full bloom.

When we were young and going out anywhere, my dad would remind my brother, sister and me to behave well by saying, 'Now remember who you are and to whom you belong.' Today, remember who you are: you are a child of God, a son or daughter of the King of kings. You have a new nature; you have been brought into God's kingdom; you owe no loyalty to Satan. One day who you are and to whom you belong will be obvious for everyone to see; your royal status will be unmistakable. In the meantime, live up to your high calling. In the Holy Spirit's power, live as a child of God and don't allow Satan a foothold in your life. You belong to a new kingdom, with a new nature, new values and a new purpose. Today, 'remember who you are and to whom you belong.'

Day 26

Read 1 Thessalonians 5:1–11

Key verses: 1 Thessalonians 5:6–11

....

⁶So then, let us not be like others, who are asleep, but let us be awake and sober. ⁷For those who sleep, sleep at night, and those who get drunk, get drunk at night. ⁸But since we belong to the day, let us be sober, putting on faith and love as a breastplate, and the hope of salvation as a helmet. ⁹For God did not appoint us to suffer wrath but to receive salvation through our Lord Jesus Christ. ¹⁰He died for us so that, whether we are awake or asleep, we may live together with him. ¹¹Therefore encourage one another and build each other up, just as in fact you are doing.

What if, on the day Jesus returns, you are having a bad day, spiritually speaking? On Sunday, of course, you were full of enthusiasm, but on the day he returns you are having a spiritual day off. What will happen to you?

Of course, Paul urges us, who belong to the day, to live like people of the light – to be clear-headed and spiritually alert. He says we shouldn't be sleeping. Here 'sleep' is not a reference to a believer's death (as in 1 Thessalonians 4:13) but natural sleep and moral laxity (see Mark 13:36). We are no longer in darkness by circumstance or nature. We have a new position, a new loyalty – and now a new responsibility, to moral alertness.

This doesn't mean we must make dramatic preparations for Christ's return, but we do have to put our armour on! We are to put on faith and love as a breastplate and the hope of salvation as a helmet. This is the third time in this letter that Paul urges us to be people of faith, hope and love. This armour is the characteristic hallmark of believers. It is what equips us to go on trusting God, come what may, and living in the obedience of faith.

We know all this. But what happens if we are just having an off day when Christ returns?

The good news is that our great confidence in relation to Jesus' return is not connected with anything that we do or are, but with what God in Christ has done for us. We have been appointed eternally for the personal and full possession of salvation, through Jesus' death. His death covers all our sins, including the sins of laxness that make us unfit for his return.

Stop seeing your quiet times, prayer life or church service as bargaining chips to get into God's good books. When Christ returns, you will be able to stand in his presence not because of your good deeds or spiritual exercises, but because of the robes of right-eousness given to you by God.

Inevitably there will be spiritual 'off days' when you are not as alert or focused on God as you should be. But don't let these days knock you off course. Remember that 'you belong to the day', you are 'in Christ' and your relationship with God is eternally secure. There is nothing you can do to make God love you any more and nothing you can do to make him love you any less.

So don't wait to give God grand displays of devotion, but seek to obey him in the regular routines of life. Today put your armour on and keep pressing on in faith, love and hope.

Day 27

Read 1 Thessalonians 5:12–22
Key verses: 1 Thessalonians 5:12–13

....

[12] Now we ask you, brothers and sisters, to acknowledge those who work hard among you, who care for you in the Lord and who admonish you. [13] Hold them in the highest regard in love because of their work. Live in peace with each other.

Have misunderstanding and arguments with leaders ever caused dissension in your church? If you are a leader, have you ever been hurt by the words or actions of church members?

Interestingly, when Paul talks about living for the day of the Lord, and describing what living in faith, hope and love means in practice, the first item on his agenda is church leadership.

There is no such thing in the New Testament as a church without leaders, or a church with only one leader. We don't know much detail about their role except that there was a distinct emphasis on teaching and ministering the Word.

In this section, Paul gives us three commands: to acknowledge the leaders who work among you; to esteem them highly because of their work (not because of personal attachment); and to respond to their leadership by creating a peaceful community.

Paul was adamant that brotherly love in the church doesn't do away with leadership, and that having leaders should not create dissent. They are to work hard, to offer Christlike leadership and to 'admonish you'. The word 'admonish' conveys the idea of tender loving care with a little bit of grit – rebuke where necessary, offering direction when necessary, but doing so with tender loving care. That is leadership.

Authority is rarely respected these days. So perhaps it seems strange that the first evidence of our pressing on in faith, hope and love is how we treat our leaders. How well are you doing in this area?

• Do you bristle at the first sign of admonition?

• Are you anxious to make their lives easier by living in peace?

- In what practical ways do you esteem them?

- Do you support them because of personal attachment or because of the work they do?

If you are a leader, consider the following:

- Are you working hard for the good of the church?

- Are you prepared to admonish others, even when it makes you unpopular?

- Is there sufficient evidence of Christlike servant leadership?

Whether you are a leader or a church member, pray through what it means for you to 'Live in peace with each other'.

Day 28

Read 1 Thessalonians 5:12–22
Key verses: 1 Thessalonians 5:14–18

....

¹⁴*And we urge you, brothers and sisters, warn those who are idle and disruptive, encourage the disheartened, help the weak, be patient with everyone.* ¹⁵*Make sure that nobody pays back wrong for wrong, but always strive to do what is good for each other and for everyone else.*

¹⁶*Rejoice always,* ¹⁷*pray continually,* ¹⁸*give thanks in all circumstances; for this is God's will for you in Christ Jesus.*

Mark Twain is credited with saying, 'It is not the things I don't understand in the Bible which trouble me, it is the things I do understand.'

These nine commands are quite troubling. There is no mistaking that they are non-negotiable – Paul starts the section by writing 'we urge you' and ends with 'this is God's will for you in Christ Jesus'. Also there are seven references to an unqualified obligation: we are to be like this to everybody, all the time.

What are these traits which should mark our lives? Paul gives three groups of commands.

1. *Minister to each other.* We are to warn those who do not contribute to the fellowship or who are disruptive. The word 'warn' is the same word used in 1 Thessalonians 5:12: tender loving care with a pinch of grit. While the leaders demonstrate this, they are not separate from the congregation, rather an example of what a Christian is to be like. So it is not left only to the leaders to show tender loving care, but also to those who are alongside them. Where necessary, this will mean rebuke and re-direction. We are also to encourage the disheartened – those who are depressed and don't have the energy to deal with life – and help the weak.

2. *Live out a Christlike character.* We have to be patient. If the word 'long-tempered' existed, it would fit perfectly here. We are not to retaliate. We are to be people of unparalleled goodness, always pursuing what is good for others.

3. *Hold on to God in all circumstances.* Circumstances are often such that it is impossible to rejoice or give thanks. Notice that Paul doesn't say 'Give thanks for everything',

but 'in everything give thanks'. No matter what the circumstances are, or what we are suffering, Jesus hasn't changed. Salvation, the Scriptures, heaven and the second coming haven't changed. This is a command calling us to live spiritually: to live consciously in the light of spiritual truth, to fill our minds constantly with the work of salvation, to renew ourselves in the presence of the Holy Spirit, to rejoice in the Holy Scriptures, to thank God for Christian fellowship, to attend Communion, to look forward constantly to Jesus. When the going is rough, this is the last thing we feel like doing, but it is a great discipline.

And notice that right at the heart of this command to live spiritually is 'pray without ceasing'. That is to say, face the whole of life – its infinite variety, all its seemingly impossible demands, our needs and necessities – in the place of prayer. Because when we are not able, God is supremely able.

Today, will you hold on to God and give him thanks? As you minister to and with people in your church, as you have opportunities to practise patience and goodness, as you deal with all sorts of trials and suffering, will you determine to give thanks to God? If it helps, take time to write down everything for which you are thankful.

There may be little about your circumstances that is praiseworthy, but give God thanks for Jesus, your salvation, the Word of God in your hands and the promises it contains. Today, try deliberately pausing once every hour to give God thanks. Be intentional about looking for reasons to be grateful and praise God.

Day 29

Read 1 Thessalonians 5:12–22
Key verses: 1 Thessalonians 5:19–22

....

[19] Do not quench the Spirit. [20] Do not treat prophecies with contempt [21] but test them all; hold on to what is good, [22] reject every kind of evil.

When we read verses like 1 Thessalonians 5:14–18, commanding us to 'give thanks in all circumstances', it is tempting to roll our eyes and mutter, 'Yes, but Paul didn't know what I have to deal with!'

But think about Paul's circumstances. He wasn't living in an ivory tower wrapped in cotton wool. He had just been flogged in Philippi. He had the marks on his body. If we find it a tall order to minister to others, live out a Christ-like character and hold on to God in all circumstances, doubtless Paul did too. So who is on our side and what do we have going for us? Paul reminds us that we have:

The Holy Spirit. The Holy Spirit here is pictured as fire (see also Matthew 3:11–12; Acts 2:1–4). His job is to create for God a clean, pure and holy people. The fire of the Holy Spirit is the fire that creates that holiness.

The Bible. In Paul's day, the churches only had the Old Testament, but even that wasn't in everyone's hands. So God used prophecy to bring the Word of God to the people of God. Mostly this was words of declaration, but sometimes it was prediction. For us, the Word of God is complete, so in a fundamental sense we don't need prophecy. But even if someone said, 'I have a word of God for you', we would still test it by Scripture. We are to be Bible people, listening intently and applying God's Word to our lives.

Our moral commitment. Whether a word of prophecy comes to you in church, a thought occurs to you in your quiet time, or you are wondering whether a certain course of action is right – whatever has to do with living the life of Christ on earth – test it. Be a discerning believer, exercise your God-given faculty of criticism, bring it back to the touchstone of Scripture, pray about it, ask the Holy Spirit to illuminate you about it. And once you have come to a conclusion as to what is right and what is wrong, then go for it!

Reread God's commands in verses 14–18, slowly and deliberately. Which ones do you struggle with most? Stop trying to be obedient in your own strength – that is doomed to failure! Today, ask the Holy Spirit to refine, purify and create holiness in you. Spend time reading the Scriptures and applying them to your own life. Be intentional as you go through the day, and test everything: your choices, your actions, your thoughts. Pray about them and see if they align with Scripture.

God did not intend you to go on this journey of faith alone. He has given these means of grace to equip you to move forward with conviction. Meditate on his promise: 'His divine power has given us everything we need for a godly life through our knowledge of him who called us by his own glory and goodness' (2 Peter 1:3).

Day 30

Read 1 Thessalonians 5:12–28
Key verses: 1 Thessalonians 5:23–28

....

> 23 May God himself, the God of peace, sanctify you through and through. May your whole spirit, soul and body be kept blameless at the coming of our Lord Jesus Christ. 24 The one who calls you is faithful, and he will do it.
>
> 25 Brothers and sisters, pray for us. 26 Greet all God's people with a holy kiss. 27 I charge you before the Lord to have this letter read to all the brothers and sisters. 28 The grace of our Lord Jesus Christ be with you.

Paul never ends his letters, 'with warm good wishes'. Even his signing-off packs a punch!

He reminds the Thessalonians to be:

- a praying church – 'brothers and sisters pray for us'
- a loving church – 'greet all God's people with a kiss'

- a Bible-loving church – 'have this letter read'
- a church founded, kept and nourished in grace – 'the grace of our Lord Jesus Christ be with you'.

How could the Thessalonians, how can we, live up to such exacting standards? Paul reminds us, above all, that we have God himself on our side. Often we feel that the task is beyond us, that we will never be ready for Jesus when he returns. But the Bible promises that God will sanctify you. He will preserve you, in an all-embracing, completed holiness that touches every part of your being and covers all that you are. This is what 'sanctify' and 'keep' mean here: he will preserve you in relation to himself, your spirit; he will preserve you in your personality, your soul; he will preserve you in holy living in your body. Our faithful and all-sufficient God will sanctify and keep you ready for Christ's return.

Even today, God will fulfil his promise to sanctify and keep you. His methods are unorthodox. He uses suffering and trials, devoted church service, the encouragement and example of other believers, and all the various strands of our lives to sanctify us.

Paul reminds us: 'He who began a good work in you will go on putting the finishing touches to it until the day of

Christ' (Philippians 1:6, paraphrased). Be conscious as you go through your day that God is using circumstances, pain, conversations and choices to sanctify you. Keep your eyes open and look out for these finishing touches. Don't resist his work. Instead, see any challenges to your comfort and priorities, any trials, any admonition from church friends, as getting you ready, so that there will be no single blemish to spoil Jesus' return.

Join Paul, the Thessalonians and countless other believers today as you speed the return of Christ.

For further study

If you would like to do further study on 1 Thessalonians, the commentaries listed here may be useful.

- James H. Grant Jr and R. Kent Hughes, *1–2 Thessalonians: The Hope of Salvation*, Preaching the Word (Crossway, 2015).

- Gene L. Green, *The Letters to the Thessalonians*, The Pillar New Testament Commentary (IVP, 2009).

- Richard Mayhue, *1 & 2 Thessalonians: Triumphs and Trials of a Consecrated Church*, Focus on the Bible (Christian Focus, 1999).

- Leon Morris, *1 and 2 Thessalonians*, Tyndale New Testament Commentaries (IVP, 2009).

- John Stott, *The Message of Thessalonians: Preparing for the Coming King*, The Bible Speaks Today (IVP, 1991).

KESWICK MINISTRIES

Our purpose

Keswick Ministries is committed to the spiritual renewal of God's people for his mission in the world.

God's purpose is to bring his blessing to all the nations of the world. That promise of blessing, which touches every aspect of human life, is ultimately fulfilled through the life, death, resurrection, ascension and future return of Christ. All of the people of God are called to participate in his missionary purposes, wherever he may place them. The central vision of *Keswick Ministries* is to see the people of God equipped, encouraged and refreshed to fulfil that calling, directed and guided by God's Word in the power of his Spirit, for the glory of his Son.

Our priorities

Keswick Ministries seeks to serve the local church through:

- *Hearing God's Word*: the Scriptures are the foundation for the church's life, growth and mission, and *Keswick Ministries* is committed to preach and teach God's Word in a way that is faithful to Scripture and relevant to Christians of all ages and backgrounds.

- *Becoming like God's Son*: from its earliest days the Keswick movement has encouraged Christians to live godly lives in the power of the Spirit, to grow in Christlikeness and to live under his lordship in every area of life. This is God's will for his people in every culture and generation.

- *Serving God's mission*: the authentic response to God's Word is obedience to his mission, and the inevitable result of Christlikeness is sacrificial service. *Keswick Ministries* seeks to encourage committed discipleship in family life, work and society, and energetic engagement in the cause of world mission.

Our ministry

Keswick: the event. Every summer the town of Keswick hosts a three-week Convention, which attracts some 15,000 Christians from the UK and around the world. The event provides Bible teaching for all ages, vibrant worship, a sense of unity across generations and denominations, and an inspirational call to serve Christ in the world. It caters for children of all ages and has a strong youth and young adult programme. And it all takes place in the beautiful Lake District – a perfect setting for rest, recreation and refreshment.

- **Keswick: the movement**. For 140 years the work of Keswick has impacted churches worldwide, and today the movement is underway throughout the UK, as well as in many parts of Europe, Asia, North America, Australia, Africa and the Caribbean. *Keswick Ministries* is committed to strengthen the network in the UK and beyond, through prayer, news, pioneering and cooperative activity.

- **Keswick resources**. *Keswick Ministries* is producing a growing range of books and booklets based on the core foundations of Christian life and mission. It makes Bible teaching available through free access to mp3 downloads, and the sale of DVDs and CDs. It broadcasts online through Clayton TV and annual BBC Radio 4 services. In addition to the summer Convention, *Keswick Ministries* is hoping to develop other teaching and training events in the coming years.

Our unity

The Keswick movement worldwide has adopted a key Pauline statement to describe its gospel inclusivity: 'for you are all one in Christ Jesus' (Galatians 3:28). *Keswick Ministries* works with evangelicals from a wide variety of church backgrounds, on the understanding that they share a commitment to the essential truths of the Christian faith as set out in our statement of belief.

Our contact details
T: 01768 780075
E: info@keswickministries.org
W: www.keswickministries.org
Mail: Keswick Ministries, Convention Centre,
Skiddaw Street, Keswick CA12 4BY, England

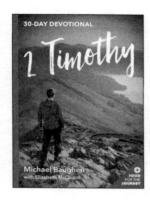

related titles from IVP

FROM THE FOOD FOR THE JOURNEY SERIES

2 Timothy
Michael Baughen
with Elizabeth McQuoid

ISBN: 978-1-78359-438-2
112 pages, paperback

The Food for the Journey series takes messages by well-loved Bible teachers at the Keswick Convention and reformats them into accessible daily devotionals.

'This helpful series will facilitate a prayerful, intelligent, systematic reading of the Bible, so that God's voice is clearly heard. There is no greater service than to promote a daily reading of the Word – God will nourish, encourage, rebuke and correct us, all to his glory!' David Cook

'A heart-warming, mind-stretching, spine-strengthening series – essential daily nourishment from God's Word for disciples on the move.' Jonathan Lamb

'This devotional series is biblically rich, theologically deep and full of wisdom that will strengthen, nourish and guide you in learning how to live life from God's perspective. I recommend it highly!' Becky Pippert

'Highly accessible and peppered with thoughtful insights and penetrating questions, these devotional guides are excellent tools to enable us to hear God's Word in our day-to-day lives.' John Risbridger

Related Teaching CD Packs

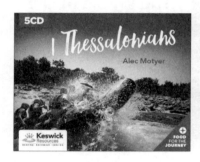

1 Thessalonians

Alec Motyer
SWP2203D

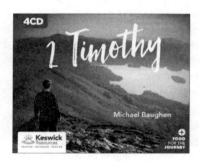

2 Timothy

Michael Baughen
SWP2202D

Available from **www.essentialchristian.com**

related titles from IVP

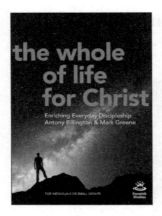

KESWICK STUDY GUIDE 2015

The Whole of Life for Christ

Becoming everyday disciples

Antony Billington
& Mark Greene

ISBN: 978-1-78359-361-3
96 pages, booklet

Suppose for a moment that Jesus really is interested in every aspect of your life. Everything – the dishes and the dog and the day job and the drudgery of some of the stuff you just have to do, the TV programme you love, the staff in your local supermarket as well as the homeless in the local shelter, your boss as well as your vicar, helping a shopper find the ketchup as well as brewing the tea for the life group, the well-being of your town and the well-being of your neighbour ...

Suppose the truth that every Christian is a new creature in Christ, empowered by the Spirit to do his will, means that Christ is with you everywhere you go, in every task you do, with every person you meet ... Suppose God wants to involve you in what he's doing in the places you spend your time day by day ... Suppose your whole life is important to Christ ...

It is.

These seven studies will help you explore and live out the marvellous truth that the gospel is an invitation into whole-life discipleship, into a life following and imitating Jesus.

Available from your local Christian bookshop or **www.ivpbooks.com**

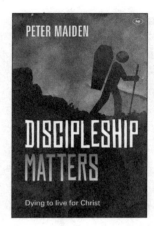

Mission Matters
Love says go
Tim Chester

ISBN: 978-1-78359-280-7
176 pages, paperback

The Father delights in his Son. This is the starting point of mission, its very core. The word 'mission' means 'sending'. But for many centuries this was only used to describe what God did, sending his Son and his Spirit into the world. World mission exists because the Father wants people to delight in his Son, and the Son wants people to delight in the Father.

Tim Chester introduces us to a cascade of love: love flowing from the Father to the Son through the Spirit. And that love overflows and, through us, keeps on flowing to our Christian community and beyond, to a needy world. Mission matters. This book is for ordinary individuals willing to step out and be part of the most amazing, exciting venture in the history of the world.

'If you want to fire up your church with a vision for global mission, this is your book! ... It should carry a spiritual health warning.'
David Coffey OBE

'I am sure this book will provoke many to respond to the challenge as they realize that there are still thousands waiting to be introduced to the Saviour.' Helen Roseveare

related titles

Knowing God Better

The Vision of the Keswick Movement
Jonathan Lamb

ISBN: 978-1-78359-369-9
112 pages, paperback

It's a remarkable story. It spans 140 years and crosses cultures and continents.

It has revolutionized hundreds of thousands of lives and it has had a radical impact on churches and communities. It has launched new mission movements and pushed forward the frontiers of the gospel. And it continues to grow, as Christians the world over see the urgent need for spiritual renewal.

Why has this happened? What are the marks of this spiritual movement? In *Knowing God Better*, Jonathan Lamb introduces the big priorities that shape the Keswick movement, priorities that are essential for the well-being of Christians and local churches around the world today.

'An inspiring reminder of biblical principles that should be in the heart of every disciple of Jesus Christ.' Elaine Duncan

'A heart-warming and soul-stirring introduction to a ministry and movement that seeks to bring glory to God by serving the church.' Liam Goligher

Available from your local Christian bookshop or **www.ivpbooks.com**